ROADMAP TO GOOD RIDES

Roadmap to Good Rides

HOW TO CHOOSE THE BEST USED VEHICLE FROM A MECHANIC'S PERSPECTIVE

Chris Fast

LogRog Publishing

Contents

First Printing, 2023

Published by LogRog Publishing, Rogersville, Missouri
ISBN: 9798218127343

Cover design by Chris Fast

Introduction

It is simply amazing how vehicles used for personal transportation have transformed over just the last ten years, let alone since the first autos were produced in America in the early years of the 20th century. I have watched some of the most significant changes firsthand from the time I started having a serious interest in being an automobile mechanic. This interest took place shortly after securing my driver's license at the first opportunity following my 16th birthday. From that point on, I have been mesmerized by these amazing machines we call automobiles.

Many of the advancements made over the years have been monumental in improving safety, reliability, and efficiency. Some of these technological realities have had a direct impact on my career—a career which includes working in the automotive and truck repair industry for two and a half decades. Some of the changes were heartily welcomed when they came. Others were, and in some cases continue to be, a real headache for most mechanics and an incredible expense for many vehicle owners. Still, working in this industry has provided a particular level of insight that can be very beneficial for those seeking to purchase a pre-owned vehicle. That experience includes holding various positions which range from a lube technician (glorified title for someone who performs oil changes), to a mechanic, a parts coordinator, shop supervisor, fleet manager, and my current position as Director of Fleet Management (this may yet be another glorified title, but let's just keep that secret between you and me). In my current role, I manage a fleet which well exceeds 700 assets and includes mowers, boats, backhoes, SUVs, pickups, dump trucks, cranes, digger derrick trucks, trailers, and several other items which burn gasoline, diesel, and natural gas. As you may have guessed, the fleet that I manage also has several assets that run completely on electricity.

Each of the various positions I have held within the automobile and truck repair industry has provided multiple vantage points along the way. These points of interest, if you will, serve as scenic overlooks that I believe can help guide those who are seeking to purchase a used vehicle. At this point, it is helpful for the reader to understand that my aim is specifically tailored to addressing key ideas, from a mechanic's perspective, to consider when the time comes to purchase a used automobile or truck. Also, I do not cover aspects related to new car purchases. Though, if that is your aim and you have found yourself reading this publication, I would strongly encourage you to continue. This is because the information will, very likely, be valuable to you in the future.

My hope is that what you find within the pages of this brief book will not only be valuable to you, but that these concepts will also be memorable. After all, if the tips are not easily remembered, they will generally not be much help when all is said and done. It is along these lines that I have tried to focus on keeping my thoughts as concise as possible for the topic at hand. At the end of the book, I have compiled a checklist of sorts which can be used to walk the reader through the main points during the process of either discussing these ideas with others or for utilizing the topics during the purchase of a used vehicle. Additionally, each chapter concludes with a review section to revisit highlights of the material covered.

Illustrations are another item that should be addressed at some point and here is as good a place as any for that topic. I would love to have put together a publication that sported up to date, colorful, nice sized illustrations or pictures to help the reader. This would be especially helpful in the sections on inspecting a vehicle of interest by giving locations of components and displaying the consistency, color, and condition of the fluids that will be examined. However, there are two primary hurdles to including illustrations and pictures in a book like this one. The first hurdle is that locations of components change significantly depending on the year, make, and model of the vehicle being described. Therefore, many different images would need to be included. Furthermore, if only generic images were used as examples, they would likely not provide enough accuracy to be of much help. This is due to the vast array of engine options and component configurations that manufactures use. It seems manufacturers are constantly changing where items are located or accessed. The best help I can offer the reader is to simply suggest that you research the engine or component location online for a specific model. If available, the owner's manual is always the best resource for learning about the layout of components and details about the specific vehicle in question.

The second reason images are difficult is due to cost. Ideally, I would like to keep the publishing cost as low as possible while the book is in its infancy.

Finally, I would like to thank you for purchasing this book! I am grateful that you have invested in what I have learned while working in an industry I love. Additionally, I would like to say thank you on behalf of my lovely wife Jill and our four children: Macy, Isaac, Claire, and Jesse. Finally, and most importantly, you should know the heart of why this writing project has become a reality: Jesus Christ! As I seek to serve Him, the King of all Kings, I must do that which is consistent with loving my neighbor as myself (Matt. 22:39). I must treat others as I would want to be treated (Matt. 7:12). This is the context for my personal interest in this book. I realize that the world of used vehicles is not only a very mysterious place for many, but that it is also quite scary. Much of my goal here is to alleviate a great deal of fear for those who have no mechanical background, experience, or training. I trust these pages will serve to replace the fear and anxiety related to the risks of used car buying with confidence that good used cars can be had. By following the simple guidelines in this book, you will be well on your way to finding one.

1

First Things First

What the Reader Should Expect

Perhaps you bought this book because you have started down the road toward your very first vehicle purchase and you have no idea where to start. Or maybe you have purchased many vehicles and, having been burned a time or two, would like to have an edge when the time comes for picking out your next ride. In either case, I am confident the tips in this book will be of great benefit to you! As mentioned in the introduction, the aim of this book focuses on things that should be considered when purchasing a pre-owned vehicle. These points come from various perspectives I have gained from working in the automobile and truck repair industry for two and a half decades. This gives the reader a unique advantage by providing insight and understanding from a mechanical and technological context. Therefore, the priorities of the guidance found here tend to focus on **reliability**, **quality**, and **longevity**.

With the ever-increasing costs of new vehicles, we have even more reason to shop in the used market. Furthermore, supply chain complications initially caused by COVID related lockdowns, quarantines, and other safety related protocols have further threatened the availability of new products across the global economy, not the least of which include passenger cars and trucks. For these reasons, it is even more necessary for the reader to make use of the material in this book for the best results when purchasing a pre-owned vehicle. If done wisely, the likelihood increases greatly that a used vehicle can be purchased which will prove to be a great asset suited for many years of useful life to the owner. That is my aim, and the recommendations revealed in this book are the means to accomplish that goal!

One additional point of clarity is needed before we start. This book is not focused on the differences between leasing vs. purchasing. In this book, I do not breach the topic of the percentage of markup you can expect from retail sellers of used cars versus buying a car from an individual owner.

Nor will you find advice given on a particular make of vehicle being better or worse than other makes. Professionally speaking, I certainly have my preferences. Those preferences are a combination of my own driving and mechanical experience as well as the result of having direct oversight and responsibility for literally every aspect of operating a fleet of well over 700 vehicles and pieces of equipment. Every make of vehicle has models that did well at certain times and models that did poorly. This statement applies both to success in sales and success in build quality. For our purposes here, my goal is to give you the information necessary to be able to determine which vehicle, out of a row of similar vehicles, will be the best pick primarily by observing and testing physical and mechanical elements of the vehicle in question.

Additionally, the following explanations and instructions are plain and straightforward. Great effort has been taken to avoid being particularly boring and to avoid getting bogged down in "technical speak." In fact, the information in this book is expressed in basic terms which can be applied by just about anyone.

What to Consider First When Shopping for a Used Car or Truck:

Application of Use

The first thing to get settled in your mind, as we begin this journey, is the application of use that you intend for your vehicle. What should the seating capacity be? Should it be a compact, mid-size, or full-size sedan? Is a pick-up what you are after because you will be utilizing it as much for part time work as you will be using it for your primary mode of transportation? Is there a possibility of kids in your future?

Children will certainly affect the seating capacity needs of a vehicle. I like two door convertibles as much as the next guy, but a Mazda Miata, for example, is going to be practically useless if a child in general comes along and twins in particular. These are the kinds of questions you will have to work through and answer for yourself. Additionally, these questions need to be asked within the framework of short, intermediate, and long-term contexts. A Miata might do for now and for the next 12 months, but will it do for the next three to five years? How about beyond that? Spend some time and think about what kind of vehicle you could purchase and make effective use of for the next seven to ten years. Why do I recommend that? Because having the same vehicle for that length of time saves you the hassle and risk of buying something more often. The longer you own the same vehicle, the more history and knowledge you will gain and acquire about that vehicle. After some time goes by, you will begin to learn about that automobile or truck, and what you learn will be a great benefit to you. It is a lot like living in the same geographic area for a while. When living in an area for several years, you become more established and confident about the area. However, when moving to a new area, everything becomes unfamiliar again. New street names and locations must be learned. New grocery stores, banks, and filling stations need to be rediscovered. Avoiding the process of unnecessarily having to learn everything all over again has value. Maximizing the value in a vehicle purchase is something we want to accomplish from the very start. In our fast-paced, on-demand culture, it may be tempting not to give the application of use much consideration when purchasing a vehicle. I had a boss who used to say, "Good things take time, and great things take longer." A good decision on the topic of how you will use a vehicle in the next seven to ten years is going to take time. Shortcuts are rarely worth it. A used vehicle purchase is worth taking your time to think through.

While we are on the topic of getting things right from the start, let's get something straight: for most of us, vehicles are a terrible investment! Consider that most new vehicles depreciate so rapidly in value that in 15 years they are only worth a fraction of what was paid for them when they were new. I realize there are exceptions to this rule. However, in a broad sense, this experience continues to prove true. Part of our goal should be to take advantage of that reality when shopping for a used car or truck. I recommended earlier to think about how the vehicle would be used over the next seven to ten years. I am also going to recommend we keep that same timeframe for the age of the vehicle we are shopping for in the used market. Why do I recommend that timeframe? First, it is easy to remember. Seven to ten years was the timeframe given for thinking through application of use. Seven to ten years also becomes what we are looking for in the pre-owned market for the age of the used vehicle to be purchased. Second, it is because a large part of the vehicle's value will have depreciated by that point. However, mechanically speaking, if a vehicle was maintained reasonably well, the likelihood it still has a lot of useful life left in it is very strong. In essence, it is old enough to be much more affordable, but not too old to be completely worn out.

Clearly, the amount of mileage that has been put on the vehicle comes into play here in a big way. Still, for now, let's imagine the vehicle's mileage was average for its age. Typically, average mileage is estimated to be 15,000 miles per year. If the vehicle is ten years old, and it has average mileage, then it will have 150,000 miles. If the vehicle is seven years old, then the average mileage would be 105,000 miles. Ideally, we will want to find a used vehicle somewhere within these two ends of the spectrum. At this point, I would like to express that I understand there will be many readers who may not be able to afford or acquire a vehicle within this age and mileage zone. That is okay! The principles and tips discussed in the coming chapters can still be utilized—even when buying a much older vehicle with a whole lot more miles on it. If the tips in this book are followed, then it will be a much more advantageous purchase than if the recommendations were not used.

Warranty Coverage and Peace of Mind

Many of today's used vehicles can be purchased with either a factory warranty (a warranty that comes with the vehicle from the manufacturer) or some level of extended warranty (available from both the manufacturer and/or a third party) that comes with the purchase. For example, the Hyundai line of vehicles typically comes with a ten year, 100,000 mile warranty which applies to the engine and transmission (often referred to as part of the "drivetrain"). In other scenarios, a used vehicle might be sold at a car lot where an extended warranty is offered. The question you have to answer for yourself, in this area, relates to how you deal with risk. Does taking on more risk generally keep you up at night? Or, can you sleep well knowing even if something breaks, you will be able to fund the entire repair? Warranties are neither good nor bad. Really, it is a matter of where the risk falls when a vehicle needs major repair. If your personality is such that you favor peace of mind and avoiding risk, then looking for a vehicle still under the factory warranty or purchasing an additional extended warranty may be something for you to consider.

For me personally, I will probably never purchase an extended warranty. There are two major reasons why I take this position on the matter. First, I began my career at a car dealer, and I witnessed that selling an extended warranty was a great way for the dealership to make more money. The extended warranties that were sold were rarely used, and the coverage of the warranty was not as robust as that which originally came from the manufacturer. Second, I recommend employing the method shared in this book for shopping in the used vehicle market. The idea is to find used vehicles which are in good shape, have been reasonably maintained, and still have a good amount of useful life left in them. For this reason, if a major manufacturer's defect was built into the car, then there is a good probability that the problem has already surfaced and was dealt with under the timeframe that was covered under the original factory warranty.

In other words, using the methods taught in this book, you will more than likely be narrowing the vehicles under consideration down to those that have already had the bugs worked out by the time you actually make the purchase.

Technical and Mechanical Support Considerations

One element of purchasing a used vehicle that simply cannot be overlooked is to consider how much support is available for a particular make and model. When I was about 19 years old, a friend of my dad's gave me a late 1960's Renault. If you are not familiar with that brand, it is a French made car. The model I had was a good example of the need for support which was altogether non-existent. I learned in short order why he gave me that car. It was because the thing was impossible to get parts for. Additionally, there was no shop in the area in which I lived that was familiar with the model I had. This car was a great buy: it was free. The problem was that I had no access to the support I needed to repair the vehicle. The same can be said of a variety of makes and models, though perhaps, to much less degree. The fact is most used vehicles do have strong support. If your choice is between a relatively rare vehicle and a vehicle that has a much larger support network, I recommend giving special weight to that support system in the decision-making process. One easy way to determine if a particular make and model has the support is to call local parts stores and simply ask for price and availability of commonly used items. Some examples are front brakes, rear brakes, a rebuilt transmission, and a remanufactured engine. It is helpful to note the pricing of the above-mentioned parts during your research. Pricing can often tell you about supply. Let's say, for example, that you are checking on the parts pricing and availability for three different models that have your interest. While checking on those details, you notice that one of the three models has pricing that is twice what the other two models' parts would cost. This is a good indication that there may be a supply issue with that particular vehicle's parts. It is possible that the model in question was not produced in the quantities that the others were. Or perhaps there was a design flaw and the parts had to be updated or redesigned and it drove the pricing up.

Similar in nature to parts support is the topic of repair support. Local repair shops should be called to request a quote for what the costs would be for major repair work to be done on the models under consideration. Getting an estimate on having the transmission replaced for each model, for example, can further clarify any major differences that may show up in the repair support area. If an EV (electric vehicle), NGV (natural gas vehicle), or any other alternative fuel vehicle is being considered, then quotes for the replacement of battery packs, traction motors, or other energy management components can be requested to get an idea on those costs and the level of support available for that kind of vehicle as well. It is okay if the repair shop gets wise to you calling and asking about several different vehicles. Just explain to them what you are trying to do in your research before buying a used vehicle. If that shop expresses resistance, then that is a good thing! Why? Because you have just learned who not to do business with. You want a shop, or a mechanic, that is always willing to talk to you about your questions. We will touch on this topic again later, and I will give some very specific recommendations on finding a good mechanic in the last chapter of the book: "Repair and Maintenance."

The Relationship of Mileage and Age as Reflected in Price

As mentioned earlier, it may not always be possible to purchase a used vehicle in the seven to ten year old zone. Furthermore, you may find some great exceptions to that rule of thumb. One example would be a five year old vehicle that has 150,000 miles on it. That works out to be exactly twice the average mileage for the age. This kind of vehicle can be found! Usually it is the result of a traveling sales job. Of course, during the COVID pandemic, many employees performed their work from home. No doubt this impacted the used vehicle market in a big way, and newer higher mileage vehicles are probably on the decline for the foreseeable future. Still, there are many jobs which depend on heavy amounts of travel. In this example, the price of the vehicle may actually be lower than the same make and model that is three or four years older. Additionally, if the model has great parts and repair support and it has been maintained very well, then it may be a great opportunity. Even though it has a lot of miles for the age, consider that there are many things that have not aged due to the mileage: the starter, the wiring, the doors, and the interior.

One additional thing to consider is that if a vehicle is extremely high mileage for its age, it may be possible to purchase the vehicle and replace the engine and transmission altogether, and the total bill still be much lower than buying the same vehicle with average or less than average mileage on it. A great deal of research must be performed to ensure this approach is best. However, there are times when this makes sense. Usually, this approach is more suited for large expensive vehicles that have been very heavily driven. A good example for consideration would be a Chevy Suburban with a top-level trim package. I personally know of a gentleman who took this exact approach with this particular make and model and, when the figures were in, he had made a sound fiscal decision.

Chapter One Review:

This book is written from a mechanic's point of view. The priorities of the guidance found here tend to focus on a vehicle's **reliability, quality,** and **longevity.**

Application of Use - A good decision on the topic of how you will use a vehicle in the next seven to ten years is going to take time. Shortcuts are rarely worth it. A used vehicle purchase is worth taking your time to think through.

Warranty Coverage and Peace of Mind - Warranties are neither good nor bad. Really, it is a matter of where the risk falls when a vehicle needs major repair. If your personality is such that you favor peace of mind and avoiding risk, then looking for a vehicle still under the factory warranty or purchasing an additional extended warranty may be something for you to consider.

Technical and Mechanical Support Considerations - If your choice is between a relatively rare vehicle and a vehicle that has a much larger support network, I recommend giving special weight to that support system in the decision-making process.

The Relationship of Mileage and Age as Reflected in Price - Even though a vehicle may have a lot of miles for the age, consider that there are many things that have not aged due to the mileage: the starter, the wiring, the doors, and the interior.

2

Choosing Make, Model, and Year

Research is Your Friend

At this point, you should have a rough idea as to what kind of vehicle (make and model) you are interested in pursuing based on how you will use it, what your seating and cargo capacity needs are, whether or not you are going to want a vehicle with a warranty, and the level of support that is available to you. How much you have to spend on a vehicle and the difference in pricing across manufacturers may further narrow the selection down by necessity. One great and simple resource to help determine which specific make and model has a quality advantage over others is to research reviews online to see what owners are saying. The following online resources are great tools for researching reviews:

www.edmunds.com

www.cars.com

www.kbb.com

All the above websites have a link on the front page of their site where reviews can be accessed. These companies have been authorities in the used vehicle space for a long time. This has given them the advantage of collecting a lot of data. Data that will serve you, the buyer, very well when it comes to researching reviews.

Once a few models have been sifted through, and the research has been done on what you believe would best fit your needs, it is time to decide on what year should be selected. There is one extremely valuable tip when it comes to picking the year of a particular make and model. That tip is something I have been giving out to friends and family for a long time. It works well and is an additional step to ensure we are maximizing every effort to purchase the best possible used vehicle that is available. What is this great tip? Well in a word: experience. What I mean is experience on the part of the manufacturer. Let me explain.

Practice Makes Perfect...Or at Least Helps

Do you remember the first time you did something, anything? The first time you made a pie, the first painting, the first time you mowed the lawn, the first time you gave a speech? How did it go? If you are like me, then it did not go too well.

Why? Experience, or lack thereof. You know what? Vehicle manufacturers are not all that different from us. When they radically change a model's body style, or the powertrain (including major components like engine and transmission) then it becomes a whole new vehicle. It may still be called a Toyota Camry, for example, but it is not even close to the Camry that had previously been produced. Any completely new body style for any particular model often produces many challenges and issues that must be worked out. This is because it is their first attempt to make a new model. It is the first run for everyone. Yes, there are design teams and engineers and so on. Yes, there are prototypes and concept cars, but they can only go so far. It is not until the new body style is mass produced that first year and everyone is driving around in it that the real issues show up. These issues are handled in recalls and TSBs (technical service bulletins). Of the two, TSBs are usually only something that mechanics see. They explain to the technicians what the common problems are for a given make and model, so the technicians can be on the lookout for those problems. The owners see the recalls as the notification of recalls is mandated by federal law. Here is what is interesting: as the new body style for a given model is made year after year, the manufacturers make improvements. Just like the second pie is better than the first, and the third pie is better than the second. With each passing year, that particular body style, which is a totally new car, is very likely getting better. Yes, there are exceptions, but as a general rule this improvement is taking place. How does this work out in our pursuit of a pre-owned vehicle? Each model a manufacturer produces will have a production run of a certain body style for so many years. Then, a new body style will replace it. What you want to do is find out what years are at the end of the production run for that particular generation of body style for the makes and models you are interested in and look for those.

Sifting through all the information to determine the later years in a production run is not very difficult. The best way to go about it is to research the make and model online. The easiest way to see the difference in body styles is to look up a particular make and model for a whole decade or more. Simply look for pictures of the exterior of the vehicle. It will become clear which years are a significant change in how the vehicle looks. Another indicator that the body style has changed is that the engine size and type will usually change when a new body style is released. For example, a quick search online will reveal that the Honda Pilot from 2002 to 2008 had the same body style, then from 2009 until 2015 a different body style developed. A completely new body style began in 2016. Therefore, 2002, 2009, and 2016 serve as clear examples of when there were significant changes to the Honda Pilot. In this example, if a Honda Pilot is to be sought, then 2002, 2009, and 2016 are years to avoid while 2008 and 2015 would be years to be pursued. To my knowledge, the body style that was started in 2016 is also still available at the time of this publication, so it would stand to reason that 2022 would also be a year worth considering because the body style that began in 2016 will have very likely matured since its inception. This approach is important and should serve as a sound guide for deciding on the particular year that makes the most sense after having already decided on the make and model.

It is important at this point to take a break! A time to stop for a minute and reveal that if you truly follow the above steps, then you are probably going to get sick and tired of talking about, thinking about, and researching used vehicles. I know that feeling myself. It is easy to simply say "Oh well," and throw up your hands and just go buy a car. Resist that feeling! That feeling is temporary and is much shorter lived than the regret of buying a real piece of junk that you are stuck with because it was a purchase in haste. If you get tired of the process, then take a break. Don't think a thing about cars for a few days, or a few weeks. It is okay. Then, when you are ready, come back to the process and start where you left off. I have made many mistakes in life that were the result of one common problem—I was lazy and tried to take a short cut. A short cut taken for that reason has always resulted in unintended negative consequences. I assure you that taking your time with this process will be worth it. The time will come when you are cruising down the road in that future great pre-owned vehicle, and you will be confident that you made a great decision. It will be then that the peace of mind of making a good decision will accompany you, and it will pay great dividends with every passing mile. Three words that serve us well in this pursuit and in life: "Don't give up!"

Chapter Two Review:

Research is Your Friend - Utilize online resources to collect valuable data about specific vehicles:

www.edmunds.com

www.cars.com

www.kbb.com

Vehicle manufacturers are not all that different from us - When they radically change a model's body style, or the powertrain (including major components like engine and transmission) then it becomes a whole new vehicle. What you want to do is find out what years are at the end of the production run for that particular generation of body style for the makes and models you are interested in and look for those.

Don't be afraid to take a step back - It is important to take a break! You are probably going to get sick and tired of talking about, thinking about, and researching used vehicles. I know that feeling myself. It is easy to simply say "Oh well," and throw up your hands and just go buy a car. Resist that feeling! Taking your time with this process will be worth it -Three words that serve us well in this pursuit and in life: "Don't give up!"

3

Exterior Inspection

What to Look for When Inspecting the Vehicle in Person

At this point, you have decided on a few cars you believe would be acceptable vehicles for you to consider purchasing. You even have the years narrowed down for each, and the time has come for you to perform an inspection on a potential candidate vehicle in person. But what do you do? What do you look for? What are you supposed to be watching for on the test drive? In one of my past roles during my career, a primary responsibility I had was to take a used car that had been traded in to the dealer and check it out from head to toe. My job was to spot any and all problems with the vehicle, so they could all be addressed one by one. It is here, at the in-person inspection process, where the proverbial rubber meets the road. It is here you must find any obvious problems with the vehicle. I can promise you the vehicle will tell you what is wrong, but first you need to understand how to best hear what it is saying. This is the goal of the in-person inspection. It is best understood by explaining it in three categories: exterior, interior, and the test drive.

The First Step

The very first thing that needs to be checked is the engine coolant level. This can be checked at the radiator fill cap. However, the vehicle will need to be completely cooled down, and the person who will give you access to inspect the vehicle needs to be notified that you do not want the vehicle warmed up prior to your arrival because you will want to look at the coolant. The procedure for checking the coolant level is discussed below (See 1. Engine Coolant below). The reason why this is brought up first is because as you begin to check the other items on a vehicle, the engine is going to be started at various times. This will cause the engine to warm up which will increase the difficulty of checking the coolant level by dramatically increasing the risk of being burned. For safety purposes, the engine coolant must always be checked when the vehicle's engine has sat several hours without running and the radiator cap is **cool enough to safely touch with your bare hand.**

The exterior portion of the inspection can be easily divided into two separate categories: under the hood and the body inspection. For our purposes here, these areas should receive the bulk of our concern and attention.

Under the Hood - Fluids

Arguably the most critical part of the exterior inspection is under the hood. Looking under the hood is absolutely essential. I know from experience: to those who are not familiar with how vehicles function mechanically, this can look like a very strange place. But by understanding specifically what to look for, the mystery and the fog of the unknown will begin to evaporate.

My goal here is not to go into great detail about mechanical theory, but rather to simplify the things you need to locate and explain how to inspect what is being tested. Primarily, the focus will be on fluids. This will give you a great window into how well the vehicle has been taken care of, and therefore, the condition of the internal mechanical components of several different systems.

The fluids that are the most helpful for you to locate under the hood are: engine coolant, engine oil, transmission fluid, brake fluid, and power steering fluid. Now here's the deal, many newer vehicles have been manufactured so that some fluids, particularly the power steering fluid and transmission fluids, cannot easily be checked. There is not much that can be done about that. In some of those cases, the unit that contains the fluid has been permanently sealed so the fluid is non-serviceable. In other cases, there are aftermarket tools that can be bought to check the fluid level and condition.

Beyond that, if you are looking at an EV or hybrid vehicle, some of the fluids mentioned in this section are not utilized. For example, a fully electric EV will not have engine oil or transmission fluid. However, it will have other fluids. Most notably, it will likely have multiple places where it uses a type of coolant in order to meet the needs of additional cooling demands produced by the traction motor, inverter, charging process, or the battery.

The important thing to know regarding fluids is what component houses the fluid and what the fluid condition should be when you find its location. In this section, we will run through what each fluid is used for and the condition it should be in when inspected. It is important to note that the locations of the fluid access points do vary from one vehicle manufacturer to the next. For details on where to find the access point for checking each fluid listed below, simply research the access point online. Then, print off a picture of the access point or make notes of where they are located for the specific make, model, and year of vehicle you are going to be looking at. Additionally, the procedures discussed below are for reference and are in general terms. To be sure of the proper procedure, publications from the manufacturer should be consulted and followed.

Engine Coolant: The engine coolant is used for a few things. First, it serves to cool the engine temperature when the thermostat opens. This happens once the engine reaches proper operating temperatures. When the thermostat opens, it allows larger volumes of coolant to circulate throughout the system. One of the components it passes through is the radiator. Usually, the radiator is located directly behind the front bumper at the front of the engine compartment and is typically mounted in a vertical fashion. At the radiator, heat energy that the coolant has absorbed from the engine is exchanged with the outside air (often referred to as ambient air), and the coolant is cooled. Once cooled, the coolant returns to the engine where it once again absorbs heat energy from the engine, and this results in lowering the engine's temperature.

In addition to coolant being used to cool the engine, it is also used to heat the interior of a vehicle. This is through a component called the heater core. A heater core could be understood as being a very small version of a radiator. When heat is commanded inside of a vehicle using the vehicle's climate controls, several things take place to begin to allow heat exchange between the coolant and the interior air of the vehicle. This warms the air coming through the heater core, and it is blown into the cabin of the vehicle to provide heat.

Finally, in many vehicles, the radiator can also have an integral cooler that serves to regulate the transmission fluid temperature. This happens when a transmission cooler is made into a radiator. Like the exchange of heat energy that is harnessed to reduce engine temperature, the same principle can be applied to cooling the transmission fluid. Once the transmission fluid is cooled, it returns to the transmission, helping to reduce the transmission's temperature.

The reason it is so important to bring some insight on how a vehicle uses coolant is to see just how interconnected the coolant is with other major systems on a vehicle. If a coolant system is not in good operating condition, then several major failures can take place: the engine can overheat and result in permanent damage, heat may not be available to the interior of the vehicle in the winter, and the transmission may not be able to cool properly, resulting in reduced performance or significant failure. This demonstrates that the condition of a vehicle's coolant system is a very important factor when purchasing a used vehicle. What compounds this issue is the fact that the coolant system is usually relatively large. There are a lot of hoses and passageways that are involved. Because of this, once a coolant system becomes contaminated or the flow of coolant gets compromised because of poor maintenance, the system can be difficult to clean.

Physically checking the engine coolant system should involve checking how the fluid looks, checking the fluid level, and checking the freeze protection of the coolant. To check the level, the overflow reservoir will have to be located and visually inspected to make sure the fluid level is somewhere between the low and high levels that are marked on the reservoir. Once the overflow tank is located, open the cap and shine a flashlight or the light from a smartphone into the coolant. The coolant should be a clean looking fluid that has a clearly distinguishable color. I will address the color of coolant in more detail a little later. At this point, it is helpful to note engine coolants have changed colors in recent years more times than I care to mention. Just be aware engine coolant can be pink, blue, orange, red, light green, and dark green. I am sure there are more colors on the way too! Why so many colors? Well, it mostly has to do with two factors:

using dissimilar metals (this is where different kinds of metal are used, i.e., both aluminum and steel parts that touch) and environmental concerns (different chemical compounds can be used to minimize environmental effects). As newer technology develops and the needs change for engine coolant, so comes a new color most of the time.

When inspecting the fluid, it will be quite apparent if two or more of the different coolant colors have been mixed. It will not look healthy. If very many have been mixed, it will look like dirty or muddy water. While some coolant colors can be mixed with minimal complications, that is not the case with others. If different kinds of coolants have been mixed, it will be very hard to tell what those particular kinds were. Therefore, all scenarios where colors have been mixed together should be treated as though the system has been contaminated. Also, there should not be any loose debris in the coolant. Pieces of material that are floating around or are clumped together and have settled on the bottom of the overflow reservoir indicate a problem.

Inspecting the radiator level is done by removing the radiator fill cap. The difficulty with this test is it should be performed when the engine is completely cooled down. This means the engine has been off and not running for several hours (if you have not read the introductory paragraphs for chapter three, then please take time now to go back and read them).

Most radiator caps can be removed by hand. Again, please make sure the vehicle's engine has not run for several hours. If this has been the case, the top of the radiator cap should feel cool to the touch. If it is warm at all, the coolant inspection cannot be performed outside of looking at what is held in the overflow reservoir. When removing the radiator cap by hand, most manufacturers require pressing down on the cap and rotating the cap counterclockwise. The cap will be spring-loaded and will often rise on its own slightly when being removed. This spring pressure is what must be overcome when removing the cap. If the cap is not pushed down hard enough, then the cap will not rotate. With inspection of the coolant, or any other part of the inspection process, don't be afraid to ask the person who is showing you the vehicle for help!

It will be important to explain to the individual who will allow you access to the vehicle under consideration that you want to look at the vehicle when it has not been running. For this reason, the engine coolant inspection should take place first as the engine and engine compartment will be cooled off for you to check the engine coolant and other fluids.

Engine Oil: The engine oil provides lubrication to the engine. New engine oil should look light amber in color when it is spread out between your fingers or put on a paper towel. When it is all bunched up in a container, new oil can look light to dark brown depending on the kind of oil and the manufacturer that made it. When the engine oil is dirty, it will look completely black. If it is somewhere in between, then it is probably just fine. If you find the engine oil to be black and thick, then the last oil change has been severely neglected. The probability, in this case, is you likely have not found the first neglected oil change. Rather, it is probably the latest example in a long line of a procrastinator's maintenance plan.

The easiest way to check the engine oil is to locate the dipstick and use it to check the oil level and condition. The dipstick is usually easy to get to, and typically the handle will be visible with either a yellow or orange handle. Simply pull it out and look at the oil on the end of the stick. You can also dab it on a clean paper towel to really see the condition clearly. To properly check the oil level, the engine should be warmed up but turned off. The vehicle should also be parked on a level surface. After the engine has sat for a few minutes without running, the level can be checked with the dipstick. To check the level, pull the dipstick out and thoroughly wipe off any oil with a rag, paper towel, or napkin. Then, reinsert the dipstick until it is fully seated and pull it back out again. While holding the dipstick so the handle is at the highest point (the dipstick should be held so it is pointing down in a vertical manner), look to see where the indicators are located on the dipstick tip. There should be a clear marking on the dipstick for the oil level. Usually, these markings are in the form of lines, hash marks, or holes. Sometimes very fresh oil is harder to see on a dipstick. If this is the case, rotate the dipstick so the angle of light changes against its surface, and the mark should become noticeable. Every dipstick will have markings which indicate the range of where the manufacturer has determined is the ideal oil level for safe operation of the engine. The oil level needs to be between these markings to ensure safe operation of the engine.

One additional tip on verifying how well an engine has been maintained is to locate and remove the engine oil fill cap. After removing the cap, simply look down into the void that is exposed after the cap was removed. It is best to do this with a flashlight or the light on a smartphone. When looking into this void you will be seeing into the valve cover. Any and all parts should look very clean. The parts may be darkened with an amber tint, but none-the-less, they should still be in clean condition. If you discover what looks like dark pudding, sludge, or a very dark rough coating on the parts, this indicates the engine has been severely under maintained. It is also a good idea to look at the underside of the cap. Most oil fill caps have a void on the underside of the cap due to how the cap was molded when it was made. The underside of the cap should be free from debris and any formation of what would appear like a white waxy substance. This kind of buildup would indicate a strong likelihood that excessive moisture is present in the engine oil. In many cases, this condition reveals poor maintenance at best and the intrusion of water or engine coolant because of gasket or seal failures at worst.

Automatic Transmission Fluid: Automatic transmission fluid is both used to operate and lubricate the vehicle's automatic transmission. The transmission is used to connect the power generated by the engine to other parts, including the driveshaft/s and axles that are connected to the wheels. In most vehicles, automatic transmission fluid (this fluid is really a type of hydraulic oil) will be rich red to light pink in color. If an automatic transmission's fluid has not been maintained well, then it will assuredly end up making the fluid very dark or black in color. If the fluid has a burnt smell, then it probably indicates the internal parts of the transmission have failed or are beginning to fail. Also, you should never see debris in the fluid. As is the case with any oil, fibrous or metallic material in the fluid indicates a problem. Like the engine oil dipstick, when available, the automatic transmission dipstick should be used to determine both the level and the condition of the fluid. Typically, an automatic transmission can be checked with the transmission in "park" with the engine idling. However, some manufacturer's procedures differ, and an owner's manual or an authoritative online resource should be consulted to guarantee the correct way to check the fluid level.

For vehicles that utilize a manual transmission, also referred to as "standard" transmission, the above fluid information and procedure to check it does not apply. While the fluid can be checked in a manual transmission, some tools will be required, and the process is not as easy. For our purposes here, if the desire to know the condition of a manual transmission is required, then special arrangements should be made with the seller, and the manufacturer's procedures must be consulted for checking the fluid level and condition.

Brake Fluid: Brake fluid, not unlike automatic transmission fluid, is also a type of hydraulic fluid. The brake fluid reservoir, on most vehicles, will be located under the hood on the driver's side of the vehicle and toward the back of the engine compartment. It will usually be a plastic container with a screw-on or snap-on style cap. One clue you are looking at the right reservoir is that the cap and/or reservoir will be labeled for brake fluid by indicating a DOT (Department of Transportation) number. For example, the brake fluid reservoir cap may say it takes "DOT 4" or "DOT 5" brake fluid. This number has to do with characteristics of the brake fluid itself. It is important to only use the DOT number specified on the cap when topping off the fluid level.

Brake fluid should be a light amber or tan color. Clean new brake fluid has a similar shade to olive oil. However, as brake fluid ages, it will attract moisture. This is because brake fluid is highly hygroscopic and, therefore, easily pulls moisture out of the air. Over time, brake fluid will attract more and more moisture. The more moisture it has been exposed to, the darker it will become. As it gets darker, the fluid will appear very dark brown or black in color. The primary thing to look for when it comes to the condition of the brake fluid is that its color tone is even throughout the reservoir. If it is not even in color, or it appears to have water or other fluids in the reservoir, then it is highly likely the brake fluid has been contaminated. This happens when people put the wrong kind of fluid in the reservoir by mistake. When a brake system is contaminated in this way, it is only a matter of time before significant repairs will likely be needed. If you discover brake fluid contamination, the vehicle should be immediately sent to a qualified repair professional so the system can be cleaned and tested. In such cases, components may need to be changed due to damage from contamination.

Checking the brake fluid level is usually easy as most reservoirs are made with a low and high marking stamped into the side or front of the reservoir to provide a reference for the correct level. As long as the fluid level is between those two lines, then all is well. One additional tip regarding brake fluid has to do with the level. If, when inspecting the brake fluid level, you discover it is near the low marking indicator, it may be a sign the brakes will need to be replaced in the not-too-distant future. This is because, as brakes wear, more brake fluid is needed because of how the system operates. However, in these cases, when the brakes are replaced, the fluid level should come back up toward the top of the acceptable range of the reservoir.

Power Steering Fluid: Well, if you guessed that power steering fluid is a type of hydraulic oil like the oils mentioned above, then you guessed right! Power steering fluid is used to provide hydraulic pressure from the power steering pump to other steering components which allow you to easily turn the wheels of the vehicle with very little effort. It also serves to lubricate many of the components of the system as well.

If you are ever curious just how much help is provided with the power steering in a given vehicle, you can safely park the vehicle as you normally would, then turn the ignition key, if so equipped, to the on position with the engine off (make sure the parking brake is set), and try to turn the wheels back and forth. It will likely surprise you just how much power is being provided by the power steering system. Power steering fluid is generally very light amber in color and, when clean, can be hard to tell between brake fluid by looks alone. To inspect the power steering fluid, the location of either the power steering pump or a remote fluid reservoir must be identified. This is because on some vehicles the pump and reservoir are made together, and in other vehicles there is a separate fluid reservoir that connects to the pump via hoses. In both cases, the reservoir should be labeled for power steering fluid to make identification clear. Upon locating the power steering fluid reservoir, the proper fluid level can be verified by either marks made on the exterior of the housing or by utilizing a very small dipstick that is made into the underside of the cap. Consulting the owner's manual or online resource may be necessary to understand whether the fluid level should be checked with the engine running, or if the engine should be off.

Unfortunately, it may not be possible to check the power steering fluid, as some manufacturers are moving to an entirely sealed system that makes it impossible to access the system's fluid reservoir. In those cases, there is no way to get to the fluid. Theoretically, the system is designed in such a way that contaminants cannot get into the system. In such cases, the fluid used by the manufacturer is meant to last a very long time.

The condition and maintenance history of the fluids described above radically impact the longevity of any given vehicle. When possible, it is best to obtain service records from the previous owners to see the level of care and maintenance the vehicle has received. This can provide an additional level of certainty that the vehicle was well taken care of.

Perhaps at this point you are imagining, "Ok great. I have

looked at the fluids, and they are dirty, so does that mean I should not buy this car?" Well, in response I would answer: "Not necessarily." At this point, it is helpful to prioritize the fluids discussed so far. The most critical would be the engine coolant, engine oil, and the transmission fluid. This is because these fluids impact the most significant components of value. Therefore, if these fluids are very dirty, smell burned, or have debris in them, I would advise against the purchase. However, if the brake fluid and power steering fluids are dirty, that would not necessarily indicate a deal breaker in my opinion. These fluids would still need to be debris free, but because of the lesser impact on the vehicle as a whole, in terms of monetary value, I would not automatically write off the vehicle. Additionally, any fluid that can be checked can be changed and/or flushed. If a particular fluid is dirty, then the cost of changing it or having it flushed could be used at the point of price negotiation.

In addition to looking at fluids under the hood, there are also other items we should take a quick glance at while we are in this area of the vehicle: namely, hoses and belts with an additional general look to see if any leaks can be spotted.

Under the Hood – Hoses, Belts, Leaks

When looking under the hood, take the time to look at any hoses and belts you can see. Take your time and simply look. What you are looking for is any obvious cracking taking place on the surface of the hoses and belts. Because most hoses and belts use some form of rubber in their construction, they will break down at some point. When the rubber begins to break down, it will often produce visible cracks. This indicates a need for replacement.

While inspecting what is going on under the hood, it is also a good time to see if you notice any leaks. A slow leak will look more like an area that is particularly dirty in comparison to the surfaces around it. This is because most slow leaks simply make the surface of the component moist. That moisture attracts and collects dirt, so it begins to form an appearance of being caked up in one place. A fast leak will look cleaner as it is able to flush dirt and grime away because of the volume of the fluid being leaked.

After the under the hood inspection has been completed, it is time to move on to the second portion of the exterior inspection: the body inspection. We will do just that after first addressing a few things that should be considered relating to service history records.

Service Reports and Maintenance Records

A word on using online service history reports seems appropriate here. While these reports can give a picture of services that have been performed, the data from those services had to be submitted to a database at some point, or the service and repair history will not be viewable. This requires some effort on the part of those performing the service to ensure the records are accurate. Additionally, simply because a vehicle does not have such a report to accompany it does not mean the vehicle was poorly maintained. Likewise, service history data can be entered for a vehicle that is in no way indicative of the level of care or quality that accompanied the service.

The only sure way to see what has happened is to inspect the vehicle yourself. Still, service records are a valuable piece to the puzzle when they are both available and accurate.

One of the best ways to retrieve accurate service records is to find out where the vehicle has been serviced and repaired by the previous owner. If that information can be learned, then you should be able to contact the facility where the work was done and request the history for a particular vehicle using the V.I.N. (Vehicle Identification Number). The V.I.N. is available in a few places. One location is on the manufacturer's label which is placed on the "b" pillar on the inside of the driver's door. The "b" pillar is the vertical part of the door frame where the driver's door latches closed. The "a" pillar of the driver's door is the vertical part of the door frame where the hinges are located. The manufacturer's decal information located on the "b" pillar will list the V.I.N. To find it, simply open the driver's door and look above or below where the door latches closed.

The V.I.N. will also be visible on a metal tag located on the dash at the base of the windshield. To find this tag, stand on the outside of the vehicle and look closely at the base of the windshield where the windshield glass comes down toward the hood. Start from the outside corner of the windshield on the driver's side and work your way over toward the center of the windshield. The only thing that will be on the tag is the V.I.N.

Another place the V.I.N. can usually be seen is under the hood. After raising the hood, inspect the underside of the hood and look for any decal that looks like it might be a manufacturer's label. Very often V.I.N.s can be found on the inside of various body panels, including the hood and fenders. These labels are usually visible with the hood open.

Exterior – Body Inspection

When inspecting the vehicle's body exterior there are a few things that should be kept in mind regarding the finish color, paint texture, and seam widths of the doors and panels of the body. A careful eye can detect where poorly done body repair has been performed when the right things are understood. The first is that sunlight is an amazing tool. Its intensity can disclose problems and blemishes other forms of light cannot reveal. Therefore, if possible, make arrangements to see the prospective vehicle in bright and sunny conditions.

The first thing to look for is a change in the shade of the color. Walk slowly around the car and look at the color shading from one panel to the next. If a panel or door has been repainted, then the color will likely be slightly off from the panels around it. This is not a guarantee that all past body repairs will be revealed. Many body technicians are more than capable of blending colors well so that differences are very difficult to detect. Still, this is a helpful thing to look for. Next, you will want to observe the actual texture of the paint. Paint normally has a pattern to it. It is not usually perfectly smooth like still water would be in a puddle. Typically, it has some variation to its surface texture, and you are looking for those variations in a particular area that differs from the texture with areas that surround the spot in question. Finally, look at the gaps between the door seams where they open and close. The hood and trunk seams should also be inspected as well. You will be looking for where there is a difference in gap width from one side of the car to the other. For example, the gaps around the driver's side front door should measure very close to the gaps around the passenger's side front door. Another place to look is the difference from one end of a seam to the other. Look all over the vehicle and you will see seams and joints everywhere. You may never have noticed how many there are. For example, look around the bumper, around the headlights, and around the fenders. Are the seam gaps even from the start of the seam to the end? Or is the tiny gap between the panels closer together on one end of the seam than on the other end? These kinds of differences can indicate a potential area that may have been repaired. You can combine all the elements of the finish color, paint texture, and seam widths to reveal where shoddy work has been done in the past. However, one thing to emphasize here is good quality body work is not something to be afraid of. In other words, if you come across the information that the car you are looking at has a history of body repair, and it is done well, then it should not in any way keep you from buying the vehicle. Additionally, if the work was performed correctly, you will not be able to detect easily where the work has been done, and the finish will last just as long as the factory finish. Unless the vehicle has a salvage title, the value of the vehicle is not typically impacted by body repairs so long as the repairs were performed correctly. A vehicle's title will indicate if the status of the vehicle is salvage. The market value of salvaged vehicles is dramatically lower than vehicles that have not undergone the level of repair that placed them into the salvaged category.

Outside of the car's paint finish, the exterior inspection should also include making sure all exterior lights work and the lenses and light housings are not broken. This can be easily done by asking the person who is showing you the car to operate the low beam headlights, high beam headlights, hazard lights, turn signals, and brake lights from the driver's seat while you look at every exterior corner of the car. Take your time and make sure the proper lights are working when they are powered on by the person operating the switches.

Regarding looking into the condition of the tires and wheels, a few simple tips can go a long way to quickly reveal any potential issues that will need to be noted. Taking a tire pressure gauge with you to check the tire pressure (measured in p.s.i.) in each tire is a real time way of telling you if the tires are holding air pressure well. Proper tire pressure information is located on the "b" pillar of the driver's door. This is also where the V.I.N. (Vehicle Identification Number) can be found, which was mentioned earlier. Careful attention to the tire pressure details is very important. This is because depending on the vehicle, tire pressure can differ between the front tires and the rear tires.

When inspecting the tires, you will want to see that the tread is wearing evenly across the tire and that the tire has a good amount of tread life remaining on it. One of the best ways to see that the tire is wearing evenly is to use the palm of your hand and simply rub your hand flat across the tire tread. Do this by running your hand very slowly and very carefully around the circumference of the tire. A very careful visual inspection must be performed on the portion of the tire you intend on touching to ensure no steel cords are exposed. Running your hand over steel cords will easily puncture the skin of your hand. On most vehicles, there will be a large enough gap between the top portion of the tire and the underside of the fender to give you enough room for checking tires in this way. Keep in mind that the tread should not be more worn down on one side versus the other (a comparison of the inner edge and outer edge are in mind here), nor should it feel choppy like an oversized cheese grater has been run over the tire. If you notice a tire (or multiple tires) is not smooth, this will most likely indicate the vehicle is in desperate need of a four-wheel alignment. The cost of an alignment and new tires should be factored into the price negotiation of an automobile with these findings. Two things to keep in mind about tires: 1. Generally, they should be replaced as a set of four. If the tires are not a matched set, then this is not as favorable as a complete set. 2. The sidewalls and tread surface of the tires should be looked at closely to make sure they are free from cracking. All tires will crack over time (often referred to as weather checking), but tires that are newer should have no visible cracks. If the tires do have significant cracking, either in the tread or on the sidewall, this can present a safety hazard. Physically driving the vehicle should be avoided until good tires have been installed. You may have heard it explained that you can use a penny to quickly determine if there is enough tire tread on a tire for safe use. This is true. To use a penny for this test, simply hold a penny upside down with Lincoln's head facing toward you. Insert the penny into the tread groove to be measured, and if all of Lincoln's head is visible then the tire's tread depth is too shallow. In this case, the tire needs to be replaced. If when inserting the penny, any or all of Lincoln's head is covered up because of the depth of the groove, then the tread is at a safe level, and the tire can be used.

When checking the wheels, you will want to make sure to look closely around the rim where the tire is seated on the wheel. If a car has been driven too close to the curb, it will result in scuffing and scratching of the wheel where the curb concrete has encountered the edge of the wheel. This can result in a bent wheel. If a car utilizes plastic wheel covers (hub caps), the damage caused by curbing a wheel will be very clear. It will often look like something has removed the finish off the plastic in a symmetrical fashion all the way around the outside portion of the wheel cover. If a bent wheel is discovered, the only right fix for it is to replace the wheel. It is possible that the tire can still be reused by installing it on a new or used wheel that is in good shape. However, the cost of a replacement wheel, and the labor to remove the tire and remount it, should be considered when settling on a final price.

Looking over the windshield, rear glass, side windows, and rear-view mirror glasses are also part of the exterior inspection. Checking to make sure they are free from cracks is important to do at this point. Depending on the safety standards for the area you drive in, cracks in the glass may cause an obstruction of view that can keep the vehicle from passing a standardized safety inspection.

What about underneath the car or truck (often referred to as the undercarriage)? If possible, looking under the vehicle is a great thing to do during the exterior inspection. However, I know not everyone will be able to do so in a practical way.

When I look to buy a used vehicle for myself, I will wear clothing I do not mind getting dirty and will plan on rolling around under the vehicle as much as I can with a flashlight to look over everything I can possibly see. The main thing I am looking for is either clear and obvious damage or leaking fluid. Generally speaking, you will be able to see if the underside of the engine compartment is wet or if any fluids are leaking. Leaks are not normal, and nothing should be leaking from underneath a car. However, there is one exception to this. If the air conditioning is running or has been running, then there may be water dripping under the car. This is from the condensation drain tube that comes out of the air conditioning system's evaporator. This is normal. However, if it is from the evaporator compartment's drain tube, then it will be clean and clear water only.

Chapter Three Review:

The in-person vehicle inspection is where you must find any obvious problems with the vehicle - This is the goal of the in-person inspection.

The First Step - Under the Hood Fluids
    Engine Coolant
    Engine Oil
    Automatic Transmission Fluid
    Brake Fluid
    Power Steering Fluid

Under the Hood - Hoses, Belts, Leaks - Take your time and simply look. What you are looking for is any obvious cracking taking place on the surface of the hoses and belts. It is also a good time to see if you notice any leaks. A slow leak will look more like an area that is particularly dirty in comparison to the surfaces around it.

One of the best ways to retrieve accurate service records is to find out where the vehicle has been serviced by the previous owner - If that information can be learned, then you should be able to contact the facility where the work was done and request the history for a particular vehicle using the V.I.N.

Exterior – Body Inspection
- Body Finish
- Exterior Lights
- Tires
- Glass
- Undercarriage

4

Interior Inspection

Musical Chairs but With Car Seats

One of the best ways to really make sure everything in the interior is checked is to start the vehicle and let it run in park. Pay careful attention at this point. You can often tell if a vehicle has a weak battery by listening to how the vehicle sounded when you started the engine. It should sound like the engine started quickly. It is a red flag if it sounds as though it is having trouble starting or as though the engine is turning over more slowly than you would expect.

Once the vehicle's engine is running, start the interior inspection by sitting in the driver's seat. Starting from left to right, operate everything you can. If you have questions about a specific function or feature, just ask the owner or the person who gave you access to the car. Start with operating any seat adjustments by moving the levers or buttons located on the side of the driver's seat that are facing the driver's door. Make sure to run all of the seat adjustments to ensure they operate correctly. If the seat is manually adjusted, then the forward and rearward adjustments are probably located on the front of the seat just underneath the driver's seat cushion. Then, from the seat controls, reach straight down to the floor between the driver's seat and the driver's door and see if there are any controls for a fuel door release. If so, push it or pull it to make sure it operates. Then move up to the driver's door panel where the locks, windows, and mirror adjustments are usually located. Run all the controls, one at a time, to make sure they function as designed. Next, you are going to operate all the controls that are located on or near the steering wheel and the dash cluster. Windshield wipers, turn signals, low and high beam headlights, horn, hazard lights, trip odometer, and any other controls should be tested. Recall that these functions may have already been tested when you were performing the inspection of the lights on the outside of the car. However, it is important that you manually work these controls to ensure proper function and feel. While you may be confident that the lights all work on the outside, it is important that all the switches are behaving normally when being worked from the inside. Making note of any check engine lights that are on at this time is also critical.

After checking these items, continue the inspection by reaching straight up and opening the vanity mirror to inspect it. Take careful note of this item to make sure that when you close the vanity mirror's door that the light goes out if so equipped. It may require having the headlights on for the light in the vanity to work. If so, simply perform that test with the headlights on.

Next, you can move on to the center-upper dash where the radio controls, infotainment, and heating and air conditioning controls are located. Regardless of the temperature outside, take the time to operate all functions of the heating and air conditioning controls. In most vehicles, the light on the air conditioning button should remain illuminated solid when the A/C is on. This is an indicator that reveals whether or not the clutch is engaged on the air conditioning compressor in the engine compartment. If the light is blinking, rather than on solid, that is a likely indication that the A/C compressor is not working. Always make sure that the vehicle is able to produce cool air when in the air conditioning mode and that you also get hot air when in heating mode. It is important to keep in mind that the vehicle will need to be warmed up to normal operating temperature for the heater to work properly. Typically, the temperature gauge will reach normal operating temperature when the needle on the gauge is roughly halfway between the "low" and "high" designations.

After checking everything possible in the driver's area, it is time to go sit in every other seat position and test whatever controls there are in a similar fashion to what was done from the driver's seat. Simply start from your left and move around to the right in a clockwise motion both in the seat that is tested and in the way you test the controls that are available. It should look like this: sit in the driver's seat and test all controls located from left to right; sit in the front passenger's side seat and test all controls from left to right; then do the exact same from the passenger's side rear seat; finally, do the same procedure from the driver's side rear seat. Finally, if the vehicle is equipped with a third-row seat, you will want to make sure and include that section as part of the musical chair rotation. As you work your way through the vehicle in each seat, remember to try out the seat belts, cup holders, console compartments, armrests and accessory plugs. Taking a portable phone charger with you to verify operation is a good way to check accessory power ports.

At this point, you may be thinking this is a lot of stuff to try to remember. Well, yes it really is a lot! Here is a tip: you can perform this same inspection in your current vehicle or in the vehicle of a friend. If you walk through the process at least three times in a vehicle prior to the time that you will do the inspection for real, then you will look like a pro when the time comes for you to do an inspection on a car you are considering for purchase. Can I let you in on a secret? When someone sees you do all this, and you have clearly done it before because you have practiced it, the individual selling the car is probably going to be intimidated. Do you know why? Because nobody does what you are going to do unless they know what they are doing. Of course, you do know what you are doing because you are taking the time to read this book. It will be clear to all watching that you will not easily be duped. This will work to your advantage.

Lastly, there is one additional spot that needs to be checked that is still considered "interior." That area is the trunk (if the vehicle has one). Trucks have a bed, hatchbacks have hatches, and EVs may have frunks. Whatever the case may be, the area still needs to be thoroughly checked for any problems. Usually not too much is needed in a trunk inspection other than a visual look to make sure nothing appears abnormal and that the light, if equipped with one, turns off as you close the trunk lid. Making sure that there is no evidence that the trunk has a leak is also critical. The trunk should have already been released and popped open if you found and tested the trunk release control during the earlier tests. In most vehicles, the spare tire (along with all of the tools necessary for changing the tire) should be located under the floor of the trunk. Trucks often hide the spare tire under the bed, so that can be considered another aspect of the exterior inspection on those. On a truck, the spare tire can usually be seen by looking under the rear bumper and towards the rear center portion of the bed area. The spare tire change tools are usually kept in the truck cab, and more details can be accessed in the owner's manual of any vehicle being inspected if a manual is present.

Test Drive

This is the moment we have all been waiting for. It is where, for the first time in our inspection process, we get to have some fun. On the test drive we want to verify that any controls that were not able to be tested, like cruise control or four-wheel drive, get tried out. You will also want to run the vehicle through some specific driving scenarios to discover other issues that have been hidden up to this point.

It is best to drive the vehicle on a route that you are already familiar with. It is also best if the road is not perfect.

When driving over a bumpy road or a road that has had several patched potholes, there is good opportunity to see if any suspension related sounds or noises become apparent. If possible, check beforehand and pick out a route that enables you to drive over a variety of road surfaces, allows for slow speeds, highway speeds, and a variety of turns. You will also want to be able to rapidly decelerate and accelerate. It should go without saying that all laws should be followed, but I am going to say it anyway: all laws should be followed.

When on the test drive make special note of how the car sounds and feels. Does the engine sound weird? How about the brakes? When you go around a corner to the right, does it sound like it does when you go around a corner to the left? Does the car shake when going down the road at highway speeds? Does the steering wheel jiggle? These are the kinds of things that need to get our attention. If the steering wheel shakes at any particular speed, it is probably a result of the tires needing to be balanced. If the brake pedal pulsates, or the steering wheel shakes when coming to a stop (sometimes revealed more easily during a fairly aggressive stop), then it probably indicates a warped rotor in the brake system. If the car gets annoyingly loud under acceleration, then it may have an exhaust leak.

Any abnormality should be discussed with the seller for an explanation and or a point at which a different price should be considered. A good test drive will take the vehicle to normal operating temperature and keep it there for 15 to 20 minutes. Normal operating temperature will be indicated when the temperature gauge is brought up to halfway on the engine temperature gauge and the indicator stays in the middle. Typically, a 30-minute test drive will work well. I mentioned earlier that the test drive needs to be utilized for trying out any features that could not be checked when the interior inspection was conducted. The examples I gave were the cruise control and four-wheel drive if so equipped. The latter can be difficult to test, but here is a good tip. When a vehicle is in four-wheel drive and then put into a turn, the wheels will begin to skip. This is because of how the system works and the geometry of turning in a circle. One good test is to simply find a parking lot where it is safe to turn in a circle. First, come to a stop and engage the four-wheel drive. Then, begin to turn in a tight circle slowly. If the four-wheel drive is working, then the vehicle will begin to feel like it is binding, and you will hear and feel one of the back tires and one of the front tires skidding or slightly hopping. Prior to this test you can turn in a circle with the four-wheel drive unengaged to see what it feels like. There should be no resistance as you make a turn in two-wheel drive. It is important to note that this resistance will not be felt in all wheel drive systems as they function in such a way that allows for a tight turning radius.

As you have read through the various elements relating to the inspection, I trust the importance of good maintenance and quality repair has become clearer. I will take the opportunity here to emphasize that there are many benefits to taking care of a vehicle that extend well beyond simply helping its resale value or being more attractive to a potential buyer. Taking good care of a vehicle also maximizes the vehicles performance and reliability. When your ride is well taken care of, there will be a peace of mind about its condition, and the care given will contribute to its providing many years of dependable service. Sadly, it is easy to fall prey to the attitude that sees much in our world as disposable. The cars and trucks people depend on every day are no exception. However, with proper care, it is not unreasonable to drive a vehicle for many years. Now, you might be asking yourself "If taking good care of my vehicle is to be such a priority, who should I have perform the maintenance and repair on it?" Chapter five will breech this topic and provide practical tips for answering that question.

Chapter Four Review:

Musical Chairs but With Car Seats - Simply start from your left and move around to the right in a clock-wise motion. After checking everything possible in the driver's area, it is time to go sit in every other seat position and test whatever controls there are in a similar fashion to what was done from the driver's seat.

You may be thinking this is a lot of stuff to try to remember - Well, yes it really is a lot! - Here is a tip: you can perform this same inspection in your current vehicle or in the vehicle of a friend. (Applies to the entire inspection process.) If you walk through the process at least three times in a vehicle prior to the time that you will do the inspection for real, then you will look like a pro when the time comes for you to do an inspection on a car you are considering for purchase.

Trucks have a bed, hatchbacks have hatches, and EVs may have frunks - Whatever the case may be, the area still needs to be thoroughly checked for any problems.

The test drive is the moment we have all been waiting for - It is where, for the first time in our inspection process, we get to have some fun. You will want to run the vehicle through some specific driving scenarios to discover other issues that have been hidden up to this point. When on the test drive make special note of how the car sounds and feels. Does the engine sound weird? How about the brakes? When you go around a corner to the right, does it sound like it does when you go around a corner to the left? Does the car shake when going down the road at highway speeds? Does the steering wheel jiggle? These are the kinds of things that need to get our attention.

5

Selecting a
Repair Shop

Nearly as popular as the questions I get regarding buying a used car, are questions like: "Who would you recommend for working on my car?" Finding a good car is one thing, but what about finding a good mechanic? I can assure you they do exist, but they can be hard to find! Here are some specific tips on how to locate one.

The first thing to do is to research shops in your area where any and all repairs are performed. If the shop advertises a type of specialty work, like mufflers and exhaust, then that is not exactly what we are looking for in a repair garage. We want to locate a shop that is well known for working on a variety of vehicles and has the personnel to diagnose and fix a large swath of problems. If we were to put it in health-care terms, we want to find a family practice primary car care provider. We do not want a specialist or surgeon. Not yet anyhow. What you are wanting to find in your search for a good mechanic is a good generalist. This kind of mechanic understands the entire vehicle. You will not find that kind of mechanic at the tire shop; they only do tires. You will not find that kind of mechanic at the transmission shop; they do transmissions. You will not find that mechanic at the high-performance shop; they do high performance. Now, if you need tires, or transmissions, or high performance, then that is another matter. For our purposes here, we will try to steer clear of shops that are highly specialized.

When locating a shop, it is a good idea to look up reviews and ask around to find a shop that does quality work that is as close to your home as possible. After all, you will not want to drive a long distance each time you need work done if that can be avoided. Ask neighbors, friends, and family members who they use. If you are having difficulty thinking of who to ask, then consider the people you know who are extremely particular. You know, the people who must have things just so, because they pay exceptional attention to detail. If you can picture in your mind's eye who that person is, then that individual is probably a good place to start. Simply asking them who works on their vehicle, so long as they live close, may prove to be a very efficient way to pick out a shop or a mechanic.

Once you have a shop in mind, try to meet the owner of the shop face to face. This can be arranged by calling and asking to speak to the owner or the manager directly. Explain that you are looking for a good mechanic. Unless you already have the name of a mechanic from the extremely particular person mentioned above, then you can start by asking the owner who he or she would use if the owner was to have their vehicle fixed. Then, ask why the owner or manager recommended the mechanic they did. Ask about the recommended mechanic's experience and work history. It should come across as if you are interviewing them to see if you want to hire that shop in general and the recommended mechanic in particular. In reality, the shop and mechanic are both working for you. If you are not completely satisfied, then it is time to terminate their employment and hire another team. Once a mechanic has been identified, try to contact the technician directly and, when convenient, ask if that individual has ever done work on the shop owner's vehicles. If they have not, then that is a big red flag. Why would a shop owner recommend someone who they have not ever used? Well, it could be because that mechanic is not busy at the moment and the owner is hoping that you need something done. Wouldn't you know it? Right here just happens to be an available technician who is being recommended. Or it could be because the technician in question is the shop owner's nephew, and this kid just really needs some work. If you come across a scenario where a technician is being recommended that the owner is not using, then it is time to move along in your search for a good mechanic and a shop you can trust.

Skills and Abilities

In my role working for the organization where I am employed, I regularly interview and hire mechanics. I relate well to them, I understand them, I love them, and I am one of them. I also know how badly good mechanics are truly needed. As I look for those characteristics that prove to be reliable metrics for competent skills, I will catch myself coming back, time and again, to three basic categories:

1. Education
2. Experience
3. Certification

A perfect mechanic in these areas would be one who has at least an A.A.S. (Associate of Applied Science) degree in Automotive Technology or Diesel Technology, twenty or more years of experience as a mechanic, and holds at least one master level A.S.E. (Automotive Service Excellence) certification. Typically, A.S.E. master certifications will be in automotive or heavy-duty trucks. These are great topics to bring up in the conversation with your prospective shop owner and mechanic. Does your mechanic have any formal education in automotive technology? How many years of experience does this mechanic have? Is this mechanic master A.S.E. certified?

It is helpful to understand that "master" A.S.E. certification is different than simply finding someone who has an individual A.S.E. certification. Passing one test makes someone certified. Passing multiple tests will grant the classification of a "master" certified mechanic. For example: eight separate tests in automotive.

These tips will help you locate a good shop with a competent mechanic who you can trust. Like shopping for a car, the process will take some patience. However, the peace of mind that comes with taking your car to someone you can trust is well worth the effort!

At this point, it is helpful to address the topic of paying a mechanic to look over a pre-owned car. Generally speaking, this kind of inspection is not a bad idea. However, it greatly limits the convenience and flexibility that one can exercise if you have the knowledge of how to inspect a used vehicle yourself. It requires setting up an appointment, driving to the shop, waiting for the vehicle to be inspected, and then returning the vehicle. Additionally, it will cost you some money. The more in-depth the inspection, the more money it will require. By the time it would take to do all those things, you likely could have inspected the vehicle yourself and also saved the money that you would have paid. Furthermore, let's say you run into a situation where the mechanic does not have as high a priority on making sure that the vehicle is checked out to the degree that you believe is adequate. Would you like the ability to know for sure? Or be able to double check what you have been told? Having the knowledge enables you to do both if you decide to have a vehicle inspected.

Chapter Five Review:

If the shop advertises a type of specialty work, like mufflers and exhaust, then that is not exactly what we are looking for in a repair garage - We want to locate a shop that is well known for working on a variety of vehicles and has the personnel to diagnose and fix a large swath of problems. When locating a shop, it is a good idea to look up reviews and ask around to find a shop that does quality work that is as close to your home as possible. Once you have a shop in mind, try to meet the owner of the shop face to face.

Skills and Abilities
1. Education
2. Experience
3. Certification

A perfect mechanic in these areas would be: one who has at least an A.A.S. (Associate of Applied Science) degree in Automotive Technology or Diesel Technology, twenty or more years of experience as a mechanic, and holds at least one master level A.S.E. (Automotive Service Excellence) certification.

These tips will help you locate a good shop with a competent mechanic who you can trust - Like shopping for a car, the process will take some patience. However, the peace of mind that comes with taking your car to someone you can trust is well worth the effort!

Conclusion

Buying a car is exciting! Even a well-used car is still a new car to you. In a way, it is like getting to know someone. You learn where all the dents are, the quirks, the things you wish might be a bit different, and, most importantly, whether the vehicle proves to be dependable. The tips in this book will serve you well in maximizing the likelihood that the vehicle you have selected is among the most reliable when compared to other like vehicles.

At this point, having read this booklet, you are ready to start your journey on the roadmap to good rides. Remember the steps and go slowly. Pay particular attention to the topic of the application of use discussed at the beginning. That singular decision sets the course and trajectory for the rest of your research, options, and your relationship with the vehicle of your future. Take your time in the process. Be patient with yourself and don't get in a hurry. Before the big day, when you meet someone to do the in-person inspection, practice the inspection process beforehand a few times on another car. It won't really take that long, and the confidence and experience you gain will be well worth it. In order to help you through that process, I have included a checklist that you can copy, or take a picture of with your phone, in order to take it along with you to make sure all the bases get covered.

The checklist is simply a summary of the inspection process outlined in this book.

Lastly, do some research and secure a good mechanic. There is no need to wait until you buy the next vehicle to start that search. If you don't already have one, sooner or later you are going to need a good mechanic. The sooner you find one, the quicker the peace of mind will come when that discovery is made.

Now, sit back and just think of all those well taken care of vehicles that are out there waiting to be discovered, bought, and enjoyed! Can you picture them? You have the tools you need! Go get 'em!

Inspection Checklist

Exterior Inspection	Comments
Under the Hood	
Engine Coolant	
Engine Oil	
Automatic Transmission Fluid	
Brake Fluid	
Power Steering Fluid	
Belts	
Hoses	
Leaks	
Body Inpsection	
Color / Texture	
Door Seams / Gaps	
Exterior Lights	
Tires / Wheels	
Glass / Windows / Mirrors	
Door / Hood / Trunk Operation	
Interior Inspection	
Driver's and Passenger's Areas	
Driver's Controls / Lights / Dash	
Front Passenger's Area	
Right Rear Passenger's Area	
Left Rear Passenger's Area	
Third Row Seat Area (if so equipped)	
Test Drive	
Handling	
Acceleration / Braking / Steering	
4x4 Operation (if so equipped)	
Noises	

Chris holds a Bachelor of Science degree in Business Management and an Associate of Applied Science degree in Automotive Technology. Perhaps, most importantly, he has worked in the automotive and truck repair industry for twenty-five years. Currently, he manages all aspects of a fleet of vehicles and equipment with more than 700 assets. Chris looks forward to learning new things and loves to share with others what he has experienced. Seeing the need for a book like this came when he discovered that much of what was offered was not written by someone who had the technical knowledge and background gained from being a professional mechanic.

Chris also wears a few other hats: Father, husband, small business owner, lay pastor, and he serves on the Board of Directors for a local classical Christian school. He resides in southwest Missouri with his wife Jill and their four children: Macy, Isaac, Claire and Jesse.